50 Avocado Toast Variation Recipes

By: Kelly Johnson

Table of Contents

- Classic Avocado Toast
- Avocado Toast with Poached Eggs
- Spicy Sriracha Avocado Toast
- Avocado Toast with Smoked Salmon
- Avocado Toast with Bacon and Eggs
- Avocado and Tomato Toast
- Avocado Toast with Feta and Olive Tapenade
- Avocado Toast with Roasted Red Pepper
- Avocado Toast with Arugula and Balsamic
- Avocado Toast with Lemon Zest and Chia Seeds
- Avocado Toast with Tuna Salad
- Avocado Toast with Grilled Chicken
- Avocado Toast with Goat Cheese and Walnuts
- Avocado Toast with Pickled Red Onion
- Avocado Toast with Roasted Mushrooms
- Avocado Toast with Fried Egg and Hot Sauce
- Avocado Toast with Microgreens
- Avocado Toast with Sweet Potato Fries
- Avocado Toast with Ricotta and Honey
- Avocado Toast with Radishes and Sea Salt
- Avocado Toast with Basil and Balsamic Glaze
- Avocado Toast with Pomegranate Seeds
- Avocado Toast with Mango and Lime
- Avocado Toast with Cucumber and Dill
- Avocado Toast with Prosciutto
- Avocado Toast with Pesto and Pine Nuts
- Avocado Toast with Cherry Tomatoes and Mozzarella
- Avocado Toast with Fresh Herbs and Garlic
- Avocado Toast with Roasted Beets
- Avocado Toast with Bacon Jam
- Avocado Toast with Grilled Shrimp
- Avocado Toast with Hard-Boiled Eggs and Chili Flakes
- Avocado Toast with Lemon and Tahini
- Avocado Toast with Hummus and Cucumber
- Avocado Toast with Sun-Dried Tomatoes and Basil

- Avocado Toast with Shrimp and Mango Salsa
- Avocado Toast with Burrata and Balsamic
- Avocado Toast with Feta and Dried Cranberries
- Avocado Toast with Pineapple and Chia
- Avocado Toast with Caviar and Creme Fraiche
- Avocado Toast with Miso and Tofu
- Avocado Toast with Corn and Cilantro
- Avocado Toast with Jalapeños and Lime
- Avocado Toast with Ricotta, Lemon, and Mint
- Avocado Toast with Almond Butter and Banana
- Avocado Toast with Blue Cheese and Walnuts
- Avocado Toast with Salmon Roe
- Avocado Toast with Coconut and Lime
- Avocado Toast with Spicy Kimchi
- Avocado Toast with Eggplant and Feta

Classic Avocado Toast

Ingredients:

- 2 slices of whole-grain bread, toasted
- 1 ripe avocado
- Salt and pepper to taste
- Olive oil drizzle

Instructions:

1. Mash the avocado in a bowl and season with salt and pepper.
2. Spread the mashed avocado over the toasted bread.
3. Drizzle with olive oil and serve immediately.

Avocado Toast with Poached Eggs

Ingredients:

- 2 slices of whole-grain bread, toasted
- 1 ripe avocado
- 2 eggs
- Salt and pepper to taste
- Olive oil drizzle

Instructions:

1. Mash the avocado in a bowl and season with salt and pepper.
2. Spread the mashed avocado over the toasted bread.
3. Poach the eggs and place one on top of each toast.
4. Drizzle with olive oil and serve immediately.

Spicy Sriracha Avocado Toast

Ingredients:

- 2 slices of whole-grain bread, toasted
- 1 ripe avocado
- 1 tbsp Sriracha sauce
- 1 tsp lime juice
- Salt and pepper to taste

Instructions:

1. Mash the avocado in a bowl and season with salt, pepper, and lime juice.
2. Spread the mashed avocado over the toasted bread.
3. Drizzle with Sriracha sauce for a spicy kick.
4. Serve immediately.

Avocado Toast with Smoked Salmon

Ingredients:

- 2 slices of whole-grain bread, toasted
- 1 ripe avocado
- 4 oz smoked salmon
- 1 tbsp cream cheese (optional)
- Lemon wedges for garnish
- Fresh dill for garnish

Instructions:

1. Mash the avocado in a bowl and spread it over the toasted bread.
2. Top with smoked salmon, a dollop of cream cheese (if desired), and garnish with dill.
3. Serve with lemon wedges on the side.

Avocado Toast with Bacon and Eggs

Ingredients:

- 2 slices of whole-grain bread, toasted
- 1 ripe avocado
- 2 eggs
- 2 slices bacon, cooked
- Salt and pepper to taste

Instructions:

1. Mash the avocado in a bowl and season with salt and pepper.
2. Spread the mashed avocado over the toasted bread.
3. Fry the eggs to your preference.
4. Place the eggs on top of the toast and add the crispy bacon.
5. Serve immediately.

Avocado and Tomato Toast

Ingredients:

- 2 slices of whole-grain bread, toasted
- 1 ripe avocado
- 1 small tomato, sliced
- Salt and pepper to taste
- Olive oil drizzle

Instructions:

1. Mash the avocado and spread it over the toasted bread.
2. Top with tomato slices, season with salt and pepper.
3. Drizzle with olive oil and serve immediately.

Avocado Toast with Feta and Olive Tapenade

Ingredients:

- 2 slices of whole-grain bread, toasted
- 1 ripe avocado
- 2 tbsp feta cheese, crumbled
- 2 tbsp olive tapenade

Instructions:

1. Mash the avocado and spread it over the toasted bread.
2. Top with crumbled feta and olive tapenade.
3. Serve immediately.

Avocado Toast with Roasted Red Pepper

Ingredients:

- 2 slices of whole-grain bread, toasted
- 1 ripe avocado
- 2 roasted red peppers, sliced
- Salt and pepper to taste

Instructions:

1. Mash the avocado and spread it over the toasted bread.
2. Top with sliced roasted red peppers.
3. Season with salt and pepper and serve immediately.

Avocado Toast with Arugula and Balsamic

Ingredients:

- 2 slices of whole-grain bread, toasted
- 1 ripe avocado
- 1 cup fresh arugula
- 1 tbsp balsamic vinegar
- Salt and pepper to taste

Instructions:

1. Mash the avocado and spread it over the toasted bread.
2. Top with arugula and drizzle with balsamic vinegar.
3. Season with salt and pepper and serve immediately.

Avocado Toast with Lemon Zest and Chia Seeds

Ingredients:

- 2 slices of whole-grain bread, toasted
- 1 ripe avocado
- Zest of 1 lemon
- 1 tsp chia seeds
- Salt and pepper to taste

Instructions:

1. Mash the avocado and spread it over the toasted bread.
2. Sprinkle with lemon zest, chia seeds, and season with salt and pepper.
3. Serve immediately.

Avocado Toast with Tuna Salad

Ingredients:

- 2 slices of whole-grain bread, toasted
- 1 ripe avocado
- 1 can tuna, drained
- 1 tbsp mayonnaise or Greek yogurt
- 1 tsp Dijon mustard
- Salt and pepper to taste

Instructions:

1. Mash the avocado and spread it over the toasted bread.
2. Mix tuna with mayonnaise or Greek yogurt, Dijon mustard, salt, and pepper.
3. Top the avocado toast with the tuna salad.
4. Serve immediately.

Avocado Toast with Grilled Chicken

Ingredients:

- 2 slices of whole-grain bread, toasted
- 1 ripe avocado
- 1 grilled chicken breast, sliced
- Salt and pepper to taste

Instructions:

1. Mash the avocado and spread it over the toasted bread.
2. Top with grilled chicken slices, seasoned with salt and pepper.
3. Serve immediately.

Avocado Toast with Goat Cheese and Walnuts

Ingredients:

- 2 slices of whole-grain bread, toasted
- 1 ripe avocado
- 2 tbsp goat cheese, crumbled
- 1 tbsp walnuts, chopped
- Honey drizzle (optional)

Instructions:

1. Mash the avocado and spread it over the toasted bread.
2. Top with crumbled goat cheese and chopped walnuts.
3. Drizzle with honey if desired and serve immediately.

Avocado Toast with Pickled Red Onion

Ingredients:

- 2 slices of whole-grain bread, toasted
- 1 ripe avocado
- ¼ cup pickled red onion
- Salt and pepper to taste

Instructions:

1. Mash the avocado and spread it over the toasted bread.
2. Top with pickled red onion, and season with salt and pepper.
3. Serve immediately.

Avocado Toast with Roasted Mushrooms

Ingredients:

- 2 slices of whole-grain bread, toasted
- 1 ripe avocado
- 1 cup mushrooms, sliced
- 1 tbsp olive oil
- Salt and pepper to taste

Instructions:

1. Preheat oven to 375°F.
2. Toss sliced mushrooms in olive oil, salt, and pepper, then roast for 15–20 minutes.
3. Mash the avocado and spread it over the toasted bread.
4. Top with roasted mushrooms and serve immediately.

Avocado Toast with Fried Egg and Hot Sauce

Ingredients:

- 2 slices of whole-grain bread, toasted
- 1 ripe avocado
- 2 eggs
- Hot sauce to taste
- Salt and pepper to taste

Instructions:

1. Mash the avocado and spread it over the toasted bread.
2. Fry the eggs to your desired level and season with salt and pepper.
3. Place the fried eggs on top of the avocado toast and drizzle with hot sauce.
4. Serve immediately.

Avocado Toast with Microgreens

Ingredients:

- 2 slices of whole-grain bread, toasted
- 1 ripe avocado
- 1 cup microgreens
- Salt and pepper to taste

Instructions:

1. Mash the avocado and spread it over the toasted bread.
2. Top with fresh microgreens, and season with salt and pepper.
3. Serve immediately.

Avocado Toast with Sweet Potato Fries

Ingredients:

- 2 slices of whole-grain bread, toasted
- 1 ripe avocado
- 1 small sweet potato, cut into fries
- Olive oil drizzle
- Salt and pepper to taste

Instructions:

1. Preheat oven to 400°F.
2. Toss sweet potato fries with olive oil, salt, and pepper, and bake for 20-25 minutes.
3. Mash the avocado and spread it over the toasted bread.
4. Top with sweet potato fries and serve immediately.

Avocado Toast with Ricotta and Honey

Ingredients:

- 2 slices of whole-grain bread, toasted
- 1 ripe avocado
- 2 tbsp ricotta cheese
- Honey drizzle
- Salt and pepper to taste

Instructions:

1. Mash the avocado and spread it over the toasted bread.
2. Top with ricotta cheese, drizzle with honey, and season with salt and pepper.
3. Serve immediately.

Avocado Toast with Radishes and Sea Salt

Ingredients:

- 2 slices of whole-grain bread, toasted
- 1 ripe avocado
- 4–5 radishes, thinly sliced
- Sea salt to taste

Instructions:

1. Mash the avocado and spread it over the toasted bread.
2. Top with radish slices and sprinkle with sea salt.
3. Serve immediately.

Avocado Toast with Basil and Balsamic Glaze

Ingredients:

- 2 slices of whole-grain bread, toasted
- 1 ripe avocado
- Fresh basil leaves
- Balsamic glaze drizzle
- Salt and pepper to taste

Instructions:

1. Mash the avocado and spread it over the toasted bread.
2. Top with fresh basil leaves and drizzle with balsamic glaze.
3. Season with salt and pepper, then serve immediately.

Avocado Toast with Pomegranate Seeds

Ingredients:

- 2 slices of whole-grain bread, toasted
- 1 ripe avocado
- 2 tbsp pomegranate seeds
- Salt and pepper to taste
- Olive oil drizzle

Instructions:

1. Mash the avocado and spread it over the toasted bread.
2. Top with pomegranate seeds.
3. Drizzle with olive oil and season with salt and pepper.
4. Serve immediately.

Avocado Toast with Mango and Lime

Ingredients:

- 2 slices of whole-grain bread, toasted
- 1 ripe avocado
- 1 ripe mango, diced
- 1 tbsp lime juice
- Lime zest for garnish

Instructions:

1. Mash the avocado and spread it over the toasted bread.
2. Top with diced mango and drizzle with lime juice.
3. Garnish with lime zest.
4. Serve immediately.

Avocado Toast with Cucumber and Dill

Ingredients:

- 2 slices of whole-grain bread, toasted
- 1 ripe avocado
- 1/2 cucumber, thinly sliced
- Fresh dill, chopped
- Salt and pepper to taste

Instructions:

1. Mash the avocado and spread it over the toasted bread.
2. Layer with thin cucumber slices and sprinkle with fresh dill.
3. Season with salt and pepper, then serve immediately.

Avocado Toast with Prosciutto

Ingredients:

- 2 slices of whole-grain bread, toasted
- 1 ripe avocado
- 3-4 slices of prosciutto
- Olive oil drizzle
- Fresh cracked black pepper

Instructions:

1. Mash the avocado and spread it over the toasted bread.
2. Top with prosciutto slices.
3. Drizzle with olive oil and season with fresh cracked black pepper.
4. Serve immediately.

Avocado Toast with Pesto and Pine Nuts

Ingredients:

- 2 slices of whole-grain bread, toasted
- 1 ripe avocado
- 2 tbsp pesto sauce
- 1 tbsp pine nuts, toasted
- Fresh parmesan (optional)

Instructions:

1. Mash the avocado and spread it over the toasted bread.
2. Drizzle with pesto sauce and sprinkle with toasted pine nuts.
3. Optionally, top with fresh parmesan.
4. Serve immediately.

Avocado Toast with Cherry Tomatoes and Mozzarella

Ingredients:

- 2 slices of whole-grain bread, toasted
- 1 ripe avocado
- 1/2 cup cherry tomatoes, halved
- 1/4 cup fresh mozzarella, torn into pieces
- Salt and pepper to taste
- Olive oil drizzle

Instructions:

1. Mash the avocado and spread it over the toasted bread.
2. Top with halved cherry tomatoes and fresh mozzarella pieces.
3. Season with salt and pepper, then drizzle with olive oil.
4. Serve immediately.

Avocado Toast with Fresh Herbs and Garlic

Ingredients:

- 2 slices of whole-grain bread, toasted
- 1 ripe avocado
- 1 clove garlic, minced
- Fresh parsley, cilantro, and chives, chopped
- Salt and pepper to taste

Instructions:

1. Mash the avocado and spread it over the toasted bread.
2. Top with minced garlic and fresh herbs.
3. Season with salt and pepper.
4. Serve immediately.

Avocado Toast with Roasted Beets

Ingredients:

- 2 slices of whole-grain bread, toasted
- 1 ripe avocado
- 1/2 cup roasted beets, sliced
- Fresh arugula (optional)
- Salt and pepper to taste

Instructions:

1. Mash the avocado and spread it over the toasted bread.
2. Top with roasted beet slices and fresh arugula (if desired).
3. Season with salt and pepper, then serve immediately.

Avocado Toast with Bacon Jam

Ingredients:

- 2 slices of whole-grain bread, toasted
- 1 ripe avocado
- 2 tbsp bacon jam
- Fresh cracked black pepper

Instructions:

1. Mash the avocado and spread it over the toasted bread.
2. Top with bacon jam and season with fresh cracked black pepper.
3. Serve immediately.

Avocado Toast with Grilled Shrimp

Ingredients:

- 2 slices of whole-grain bread, toasted
- 1 ripe avocado
- 6 grilled shrimp
- Lemon zest
- Fresh cilantro, chopped
- Salt and pepper to taste

Instructions:

1. Mash the avocado and spread it over the toasted bread.
2. Top with grilled shrimp, lemon zest, and chopped cilantro.
3. Season with salt and pepper.
4. Serve immediately.

Avocado Toast with Hard-Boiled Eggs and Chili Flakes

Ingredients:

- 2 slices of whole-grain bread, toasted
- 1 ripe avocado
- 2 hard-boiled eggs, sliced
- Chili flakes to taste
- Salt and pepper to taste

Instructions:

1. Mash the avocado and spread it over the toasted bread.
2. Top with sliced hard-boiled eggs and sprinkle with chili flakes.
3. Season with salt and pepper, then serve immediately.

Avocado Toast with Lemon and Tahini

Ingredients:

- 2 slices of whole-grain bread, toasted
- 1 ripe avocado
- 1 tbsp tahini
- 1 tbsp lemon juice
- Lemon zest for garnish
- Salt and pepper to taste

Instructions:

1. Mash the avocado and spread it over the toasted bread.
2. Drizzle with tahini and lemon juice.
3. Garnish with lemon zest and season with salt and pepper.
4. Serve immediately.

Avocado Toast with Hummus and Cucumber

Ingredients:

- 2 slices of whole-grain bread, toasted
- 1 ripe avocado
- 2 tbsp hummus
- ½ cucumber, thinly sliced
- Salt and pepper to taste

Instructions:

1. Mash the avocado and spread it over the toasted bread.
2. Top with hummus and cucumber slices.
3. Season with salt and pepper, then serve immediately.

Avocado Toast with Sun-Dried Tomatoes and Basil

Ingredients:

- 2 slices of whole-grain bread, toasted
- 1 ripe avocado
- 3-4 sun-dried tomatoes, chopped
- Fresh basil leaves
- Olive oil drizzle
- Salt and pepper to taste

Instructions:

1. Mash the avocado and spread it over the toasted bread.
2. Top with chopped sun-dried tomatoes and fresh basil leaves.
3. Drizzle with olive oil and season with salt and pepper.
4. Serve immediately.

Avocado Toast with Shrimp and Mango Salsa

Ingredients:

- 2 slices of whole-grain bread, toasted
- 1 ripe avocado
- 6 cooked shrimp, peeled
- ½ cup mango salsa (diced mango, onion, cilantro, lime juice)
- Salt and pepper to taste

Instructions:

1. Mash the avocado and spread it over the toasted bread.
2. Top with shrimp and mango salsa.
3. Season with salt and pepper, then serve immediately.

Avocado Toast with Burrata and Balsamic

Ingredients:

- 2 slices of whole-grain bread, toasted
- 1 ripe avocado
- 2 oz burrata cheese
- Balsamic glaze drizzle
- Fresh basil leaves

Instructions:

1. Mash the avocado and spread it over the toasted bread.
2. Top with torn burrata cheese and drizzle with balsamic glaze.
3. Garnish with fresh basil leaves.
4. Serve immediately.

Avocado Toast with Feta and Dried Cranberries

Ingredients:

- 2 slices of whole-grain bread, toasted
- 1 ripe avocado
- 2 tbsp crumbled feta cheese
- 1 tbsp dried cranberries
- Honey drizzle (optional)

Instructions:

1. Mash the avocado and spread it over the toasted bread.
2. Top with crumbled feta and dried cranberries.
3. Optionally, drizzle with honey.
4. Serve immediately.

Avocado Toast with Pineapple and Chia

Ingredients:

- 2 slices of whole-grain bread, toasted
- 1 ripe avocado
- ½ cup pineapple chunks
- 1 tbsp chia seeds
- Salt and pepper to taste

Instructions:

1. Mash the avocado and spread it over the toasted bread.
2. Top with pineapple chunks and sprinkle with chia seeds.
3. Season with salt and pepper, then serve immediately.

Avocado Toast with Caviar and Creme Fraiche

Ingredients:

- 2 slices of whole-grain bread, toasted
- 1 ripe avocado
- 1 tsp caviar
- 1 tbsp creme fraiche
- Fresh dill for garnish

Instructions:

1. Mash the avocado and spread it over the toasted bread.
2. Top with caviar and a dollop of creme fraiche.
3. Garnish with fresh dill.
4. Serve immediately.

Avocado Toast with Miso and Tofu

Ingredients:

- 2 slices of whole-grain bread, toasted
- 1 ripe avocado
- ½ block tofu, crumbled
- 1 tbsp miso paste
- Soy sauce drizzle
- Sesame seeds for garnish

Instructions:

1. Mash the avocado and spread it over the toasted bread.
2. Mix crumbled tofu with miso paste and place on top of the avocado toast.
3. Drizzle with soy sauce and sprinkle with sesame seeds.
4. Serve immediately.

Avocado Toast with Corn and Cilantro

Ingredients:

- 2 slices of whole-grain bread, toasted
- 1 ripe avocado
- ½ cup corn kernels (fresh or grilled)
- Fresh cilantro leaves
- Lime wedges for garnish
- Salt and pepper to taste

Instructions:

1. Mash the avocado and spread it over the toasted bread.
2. Top with corn kernels and fresh cilantro.
3. Garnish with lime wedges and season with salt and pepper.
4. Serve immediately.

Avocado Toast with Jalapeños and Lime

Ingredients:

- 2 slices of whole-grain bread, toasted
- 1 ripe avocado
- 1 jalapeño, sliced thin
- 1 tbsp lime juice
- Salt and pepper to taste

Instructions:

1. Mash the avocado and spread it over the toasted bread.
2. Top with jalapeño slices and drizzle with lime juice.
3. Season with salt and pepper, then serve immediately.

Avocado Toast with Ricotta, Lemon, and Mint

Ingredients:

- 2 slices of whole-grain bread, toasted
- 1 ripe avocado
- 2 tbsp ricotta cheese
- Zest of 1 lemon
- Fresh mint leaves
- Honey drizzle (optional)

Instructions:

1. Mash the avocado and spread it over the toasted bread.
2. Add a dollop of ricotta cheese and sprinkle with lemon zest.
3. Garnish with fresh mint leaves and drizzle with honey if desired.
4. Serve immediately.

Avocado Toast with Almond Butter and Banana

Ingredients:

- 2 slices of whole-grain bread, toasted
- 1 ripe avocado
- 2 tbsp almond butter
- 1 banana, sliced
- Cinnamon sprinkle (optional)

Instructions:

1. Mash the avocado and spread it over the toasted bread.
2. Spread almond butter over the avocado.
3. Top with banana slices and sprinkle with cinnamon.
4. Serve immediately.

Avocado Toast with Blue Cheese and Walnuts

Ingredients:

- 2 slices of whole-grain bread, toasted
- 1 ripe avocado
- 2 tbsp blue cheese, crumbled
- 1 tbsp walnuts, chopped
- Honey drizzle (optional)

Instructions:

1. Mash the avocado and spread it over the toasted bread.
2. Top with crumbled blue cheese and chopped walnuts.
3. Drizzle with honey if desired.
4. Serve immediately.

Avocado Toast with Salmon Roe

Ingredients:

- 2 slices of whole-grain bread, toasted
- 1 ripe avocado
- 1 tbsp salmon roe
- Fresh dill for garnish
- Lemon wedges for garnish

Instructions:

1. Mash the avocado and spread it over the toasted bread.
2. Top with salmon roe and garnish with fresh dill.
3. Serve with lemon wedges on the side.

Avocado Toast with Coconut and Lime

Ingredients:

- 2 slices of whole-grain bread, toasted
- 1 ripe avocado
- 2 tbsp shredded coconut
- 1 tbsp lime juice
- Lime zest for garnish

Instructions:

1. Mash the avocado and spread it over the toasted bread.
2. Sprinkle with shredded coconut and drizzle with lime juice.
3. Garnish with lime zest.
4. Serve immediately.

Avocado Toast with Spicy Kimchi

Ingredients:

- 2 slices of whole-grain bread, toasted
- 1 ripe avocado
- ¼ cup spicy kimchi, chopped
- Sesame seeds for garnish

Instructions:

1. Mash the avocado and spread it over the toasted bread.
2. Top with chopped spicy kimchi.
3. Garnish with sesame seeds.
4. Serve immediately.

Avocado Toast with Eggplant and Feta

Ingredients:

- 2 slices of whole-grain bread, toasted
- 1 ripe avocado
- ½ cup roasted eggplant, sliced
- 2 tbsp feta cheese, crumbled
- Olive oil drizzle

Instructions:

1. Mash the avocado and spread it over the toasted bread.
2. Top with roasted eggplant slices and crumbled feta cheese.
3. Drizzle with olive oil and serve immediately.

www.ingramcontent.com/pod-product-compliance
Lightning Source LLC
LaVergne TN
LVHW081331060526
838201LV00055B/2566